Famous Quotes on Life

Famous Quotes on Life

Be like the air, smooth and unpredictable.

DR. MARK D. NORRIS

PALMETTO

PUBLISHING
Charleston, SC
www.PalmettoPublishing.com

Hardcover ISBN: 979-8-8229-5333-8
Paperback ISBN: 979-8-8229-5334-5

DR. MARK DAVID NORRIS

Be like the air, smooth and unpredictable.
It is time to do battle.
Look at my heart, not my skin color.
If I could only read one book, it would be the Bible.

PREFACE

This book looks at the world we live in. My quotes reflect on many aspects of our society. For example, my thoughts about education, religion, sex, race, government, the nation, life in general, myself, family, and love. I have always had much to say. I have often commented to my family, friends, colleagues, and many of my students that writing is the most powerful tool we have. Although our life is short-lived, our words and deeds live on forever. For example, look at the Bible. Although the authors have all long since passed, their words live on, as does the words of Jesus. Without that documentation, nobody would ever have known their genius.

I hope, in some manner, I have inspired you to also share your thoughts and feelings about the world. No matter what I might say, there might be someone that could find my words to be offensive. I have not intended for any of my quotes to be taken that way, but it is almost impossible not to offend someone. I want people to come together so we can build a better world, which links our hearts, souls, and cultures.

BEST REGARDS,
DR. MARK DAVID NORRIS

ABOUT THE AUTHOR

I was born and raised on the east coast of the United States. I grew up in the country and I was raised with traditional values. Growing up, I played various sports such as baseball, football, soccer, basketball, swimming, and I rode motorcycles. I still maintain those good old-fashioned values that made America great. I also am a martial artist, and I excelled at many sports.

I earned my doctorate degree, two master's degrees and my bachelor's degree. I have worked in education, entertainment, and transportation. I have numerous life experiences which have led to me writing several books. I am married and I have several children.

Thank you for purchasing my book, and I hope I have inspired you in some manner to go after your dreams.

WARMEST REGARDS,
DR. MARK DAVID NORRIS

Table of Contents

THINGS I OFTEN SAY

1. I keep wondering if anybody has noticed me yet.

2. Be like the air, smooth and unpredictable.

3. Perfect no, better yes!

4. A man can never have too many cowboy hats.

5. Antiques are evidence of the ones that came before us.

6. The train runs in both directions.

7. The new world has great potential, but it needs people of good character to lead the way.

8. A man can never have too many Harley- Davidson's in his garage.

9. I have often been told that I am a Renaissance man because many people have told me I am good at so many things. I truly appreciate that.

10. I am like the terminator, in that, I never give up.

11. When someone knocks you down, you can either wallow in sorrow, or challenge them to do it again.

12. A man who starts out with an honest wife, tends to have fewer problems than a man that starts out with a dishonest one.

13. It's time to do battle.

14. What do you see in your mirror? Someone with pride or someone you don't like.

15. My book is my battlefield.

16. Just as there is a road into America, there is also one out of America.

17. Just because something is legal, doesn't mean it is right.

18. It is often perception, rather than reality, that influences our beliefs.

19. We can run from anything except our own mind. That, we must deal with.

20. Any money you make in a day is better than making no money in a day.

21. There's pride in working if you earned it honestly.

22. Are we in control of our lives or do we just go through life dealing with what comes our way?

23. If you had one hour to live, would you still dwell on the pettiness of your thoughts?

24. Do you measure one's strength by the value of their bank account, the size of their muscles, or the content of their heart?

25. The greatest man I ever knew is the man I daily strived to become.

26. Little things hurt the most.

27. There is no perfection, only the thought of it we create in our mind.

28. If I had one wish it would be to…Well if I told you, it wouldn't be a wish now, would it?

29. The most beautiful thought I ever had was the mere thought of looking forward to having that thought again.

30. There is no such thing as fear. Fear is the defeat you have inside yourself. The only difference is you woke it up.

31. My body might be older, but my mind is still holding at 16, 21, 33, 44 and so on.

32. I still haven't decided if I am grown up yet. I keep waiting for a sign or something to tell me. Maybe, when I am at death's door, I will know, I am now grown up.

33. For many years, I was lost. It is difficult to find the right road when you have no idea where you want or need to go.

34. If you are going to be a dreamer, you must first be a doer. Without action, there are no dreams.

35. I don't want to go this fast, but I also don't want to go this slow.

36.   When you give into the things that haunt you, you soon realize they were not what was haunting you. It is you that was haunting you.

37.   All too often, we choose the easy road only to find out the hard road was easier in the long run. Myself, I prefer the roughest road possible. Then I can accept that I have done all that I could do. In time, I hope the road gets easier, but a rough road wakes me up again.

38.   When you are on an airplane, over the ocean, are you anywhere or are you no-where? I cannot decide. Maybe I like it like that. You know, being in between it all.

39.   I am content to be who I am. If I was anybody else, that would dismiss my own existence.

40.   Failure loves company. But success and pride stand alone.

41.   Inside me, I have a lion!

42.   A man is only as free as he feels he is.

43.   Loneliness is the greatest punishment of all. If a man doesn't feel needed, he is the loneliest of all.

44.   I wish I had the strength to help everybody, but at times, I feel like I can help nobody. Does that mean I am getting old? Or am I just plain worn out? I wish I knew.

45.   They say, what a person doesn't see, one never misses. I don't believe that, because we all think there must be something better out there anywhere but here. So, we do miss what we don't see even though we may not even know what it is that we are missing.

46. Even when I am tired, I want to keep going. I wish I knew how to relax. But if I did that, I wouldn't be who I am, right?

47. My personality is very consistent, but my experiences are anything but consistent.

48. My life used to be like a soap opera, but one day I decided to cancel the show.

49. How do I release stress? First, I growl and then I scream. My neighbors might be scared, but I feel better.

50. I am never lost because I have faith in my ability to make the right decision.

51. Think I hurt it?

52. Every town has a road out of it.

53. No man can make a fat woman feel thin.

54. You can never have too many Bibles or crosses.

55. Whose fault is that?

56. Right!

57. Let's roll!

58. See you in Hollywood.

59. I love drag racing!

60. If I had the money, I would be a professional race car driver, because there aren't too many people who can out drive me.

61. Asking for help doesn't mean you are weak; it means you have the courage to get it right.

62. Country people are so misunderstood.

63. All my heroes wear leather.

64. I will always be a cowboy.

65. If everything is possible in your mind, then everything is possible in reality.

66. I am still the little boy that saved his lunch bags just because my mom touched them.

67. I go, I go now.

68. I do what I want when I want. Remember, that has a price. Are you willing to pay the price?

69. You are always better to have too much power than not enough power.

70. Europeans take rocks and make them into cities, many others take cities and make them into rocks.

71. I say what I please.

72. Money seems to give people permission to do anything even if they don't deserve it.

73. Nothing rules the road like a Corvette.

74. I am not perfect. I have made mistakes. However, I try to do what is right. I guess that is all any of us can do.

75. You learn more about a person by what they don't say, rather than what they do say.

76. You might be a tough guy, but remember, there is always someone out there that can bring you down a peg or two. So, be humble and polite, when possible.

77. My life has often been like a race car at full throttle. I would like to slow it down, but I'm not sure how.

78. What else is there besides love, compassion, and peace? Nothing, I think.

79. What's wrong with you?

80. Be like the air, smooth and unpredictable.

I HAVE BEEN TOLD THAT I HAVE A NICE SMILE!

81. I am like a cat. I purr, growl, and I scratch. But I can be very loving as well.

82. Everything is important and nothing is important.

83. I don't want a cook, a gardener, or a maid. If I am too lazy to do those things, maybe I shouldn't own a house.

84. I don't care how busy I am, I always make time for people.

85. I return all calls even If I don't like you. I like to have answers and closure.

86. I am proud to be who I am and what I am.

87. Me, a Hollywood heart throb, I hope so.

88. Sometimes, a good old fashioned ass whipping is exactly what is needed. Right now, might be appropriate.

89. I love flash, but many people think I don't. We always appear different to people than we appear to ourselves.

90. I can adapt to many things.

91. I have moves like Elvis Presley, guts like Evel Knievel, and charisma like James Bond. I hear you laughing, but it's all true.

92. I don't dream about what I want to do. I work towards my dreams.

93. Think for yourself, or someone else will make the decision for you.

94. I love SS's and Z28's. Some of you are thinking, what is that? Muscle cars.

95. I like taking what nobody wants and making it beautiful. Then everybody wants it, but they can't have it, it's mine.

96. You can't beat the original. I am the original.

97. People often tell me; I know exactly what to say and when to say it.

98. I enjoy being hungry because it keeps me on the edge.

99. You know what a hungry lion will do to a piece of fresh meat? That is how aggressive I can be.

100. If I ever tell you I am coming to kick your ass, you better believe I am coming to kick your ass.

101. I will gladly apologize if I am wrong. However, if I am not, I will stand my ground, no matter what.

102. I would have made a good cowboy. I look good in a cowboy hat, and I am very fast with a gun.

103. I love speed, but I surely respect it.

104. On My God.

105. I don't like stinky things.

106. That's right.

107. It's all backed up.

108. Give me some of that peanut butter baby.

109. We've got to make up time.

110. Nobody called me today. I guess I am losing my popularity.

111. The faster the car the better, but that doesn't mean I need to use all that speed. It is like power; just because one has it doesn't mean it needs to be fully utilized. That is what it means to respect others.

112. My personality is a lot like Clint Eastwood in the movies. I never mess with anybody, but if they force me, I will do what is necessary.

113. Be thankful for whatever you receive because nobody has to give you anything.

114. An apology takes courage.

115. I'm like the Incredible Hulk occasionally. You wouldn't like me when I am angry.

116. Whenever you are good at something, you make it look easy.

117. I often find myself one step away from greatness or one step away from failure.

118. The faster you fall from success, the greater the fall from fear.

119. I'm not right all the time, but I make much sense most of the time.

120. How can something be beautiful and ugly at the same time? Beauty brings joy when it acknowledges you and beauty brings ugliness when it ignores you.

121. Are you scared?

122. What's your problem?

123. People often ask me, how fast is your corvette? I say, ungodly.

124. Enough said; now get out there and take some action.

125. I love the sound of raw horsepower. That's sexy.

126. Let me tell you, I worked hard and barely got bye many a day, but my drive to be successful always won out over my drive to quit.

127. If it isn't country, it isn't cool.

128. I am total country.

129. Everybody I have introduced to country music has loved it.

130. You had to have it.

131. I had to have it.

132. I am never bored because I can create something out of nothing.

133. I am a cross between Tom Selleck, Burt Reynolds, and Tom Hanks. Now, that's some good company.

134. People often say I look macho and tough, which I can be. But people also say, when they get to know me, they see the kindness and love in my heart. I think that is a beautiful compliment and I appreciate that.

135. Now that's romantic.

136. A sexy woman once told me when I smile my whole face lights up. That compliment will stay with me forever.

137. It's downstair.

138. How attractive.

139. I have been so poor at times, that all I ate was cereal.

140. They come in crying, but they leave smiling.

141. I always wanted to be a cop. But my bad eyesight kept me from it, but I would have made a good one. I would have been fair, honest, and taken that responsibility seriously.

142. I really hate to argue or make people feel bad, but if I sit by and say nothing, I feel bad about that too.

143. Even if you don't agree with what I write, I know, in the back of your mind, you think, what I say makes sense.

144. You think I hurt it?

145. You know what I really dislike is people that are always negative and quitters. You already know much of their character before you even get to know them.

146. I like waking people up to reality.

147. Even if I disagree with another person, I respect them for having the courage and respect to debate an issue with me. Maybe, we can both learn from that experience. I know I always do.

148. I always wanted to be a household name because I thought I could make a difference. Now I realize, I do make a difference. Even if very few people know my name.

149. I love the Speed Channel.

150. King Chevy!

151. I love it when people underestimate me.

152. I always attempt to respect people in all that I do, even if they don't always respect me or deserve it.

153. Being professional is an extremely important asset.

154. Never show a person all your power. Let them think you are weak. When the time is appropriate, you may unleash your power.

155. I love sports because it gives you permission to kick the hell out of someone and not go to jail for it.

156. I speak not only for myself, but for the people who don't have the courage, education, or opportunity to voice their opinions.

157. I want the good stuff.

158. You know what really upsets me? Being falsely accused of something and allowing lies to prevail.

159. Caps are cool, but if you want to really impress someone wear a cowboy hat.

160. I would rather drive an old car with class and style than a new one out of the factory.

161. Camaros', Corvettes,' and Chevelles', who cares about the rest?

162. If it's not a muscle car, I could care less about it.

163. I used to be like a bull. Now that bull only comes out occasionally.

164. I'm not going to pretend to be a saint, because I am not. I have done many things wrong, but I always attempt to do what is right.

165. Should have, would have, could have, do these words sound familiar?

166. I want a car so fast that my hair stands up on the back of my neck. Now that's exciting.

167. I love to go fast!

168. Well, hello there!

169. What do you think?

170. There isn't much I can't do. And if I cannot do it, I learn it.

171. I was an excellent athlete, and I didn't take advantage of that while I was young. This was long before athletes were millionaires. So, when I was 36, I tried out for a professional football team in the CFL. I didn't make it, but I felt as though I could. My window of opportunity had long since passed. Never let that happen to you.

172. Some people say I talk too much. That might be true, but I would rather be a talkative person than sit there like a lump.

173. People say, how do you come up with all this stuff? I tell them, I am a deep thinker.

174. Quickly, quietly, and efficiently.

175. I can make anything look good.

176. Quick, that's not quick.

177. I may not be famous, but I can compete with the best of them.

178. I will always have faith in myself.

179. I never run out of things to say. But I run out of the will to say them.

180. Give up; I don't know the meaning of that word. You always fight until you can no longer fight.

181. Nobody called me today. I guess that means I am losing my popularity.

182. Everybody has heroes, including me. We all need them, but the greatest heroes were the two doctors that saved my life, twice.

183. Baby got front.

184. I like it when things are a little dangerous.

185. I like to get it done right, and get it done fast.

186. Race cars don't have air-conditioning or a spare tire.

187. It doesn't matter how long you can do a burnout. What matters is how fast you get down the track.

188. One of the greatest gifts is being able to sing. That is one thing I wish I could do well.

189. Even when I am dead, my words will live on. That is the power of writing.

190. Finish the job.

191. I am not trying to prove you wrong. I am just trying to expose the truth.

192. Being number one is something I attempt to do in everything I do. But the journey of getting to be number one is what I cherish most.

193. I have had a few nicknames in my life: Dirtball when I was a child because I was always playing in the dirt. Bush, due to my hair when I was in high school. Don King had nothing on me. BA, because of my bad attitude as a bad ass when I was very young, and Hollywood, because I like to wear sunglasses, and people often said I looked like a movie star.

194. This notion that airing car chases in Los Angeles makes a person famous is ridiculous. It is just another idiot that is risking the lives of innocent bystanders. I think we should give the police permission to do whatever they need to do to stop these morons.

195. One can never have too much power.

196. Perfect!

197. Silence is what we think we do not hear.

198. I am the Irish Stallion!

199. I used to think, I was a tough guy. At times, I still do. Now I realize, it's not the toughness of my exterior that prevails; it is the softness of my soul that gives me the greatest peace.

200. I like to do things myself. Then I know it has been done right.

201. Even though I've been through much, I kept that sense of innocence that somewhere there was a woman that God had planned for me. I finally met that woman.

202. I want a woman that loves me like no other man ever existed. I found that in my wife.

203. I will regret it if I don't, and I will regret it if I do.

204. To be continued.

I love a Harley Davidson.

EDUCATION

205. With the new Common Core educational standards, we are attempting to teach students critical thinking and analytical skills. Yet, at the same time, we are also attempting to suppress what people say. There is a major disconnect between these two concepts.

206. An indecisive person is one that blames others when they don't have the courage to decide on their own.

207. I always tell my students, if the quarterback gets hurt, the game keeps going. Life is like that. You must be prepared, or life will run you over.

208. Education is not about showing people how smart you are. Education is about teaching students the value of learning.

209. You are very smart; you just don't realize it yet.

210. Through education and time, the truth is always exposed.

211. Critical thinking is the ability to be able to look at an issue, question, or problem with an open mind from as many angles as possible to come up with sensible and rational solutions that make logical and rational sense.

212. As a teacher, I have had students who will do anything I ask of them, and I have also had students that will do nothing I ask of them.

213. People can't wait to be out of high school, but once out, they can't wait to be back in.

214. One of my students told me I was the best teacher she ever had. This is what it means to be a teacher.

215. Another student told me, thank you for being a real man. I haven't had one in my life. I knew I had some impact on this student. I thank God for allowing me to touch this student's life.

216. There is tremendous value in higher education.

217. Maybe by encouraging someone in some small manner, I have made them better.

218. Money doesn't buy class, education, or intelligence, but the ones that have money attempt to buy it. Some of us are attracted to the people that have it, only to find out that many of the ones that have it are surely no better than the ones they attempt to avoid.

219. If I can find one positive attribute in a student, there is hope for them to find many more.

220. I hope much of what I have accomplished as a teacher, writer, father, husband, actor, and a friend will endure long after I have perished.

221. I pray that I have positively impacted the people I encounter.

222. Several of my students said, Dr. Norris you should be president. I would vote for you. What you say makes sense.

223. Listening is one of the best skills one can possess.

224. I hope, as a teacher and a counselor, I have positively impacted the students that have entered my room. If I have helped even one, I know I have done my job. I want the best for all of them.

225. Many students ask me, Dr. Norris, why are you so smart? I say, it comes from years of study, living life, and observing people. I also tell them; I have made many mistakes. We learn from all that comes our way.

226. At the beginning of the school day, the school expects all students to stand and say the pledge of allegiance. I asked my students to stand if they loved America. Out of 28 students, myself, and one other student were the only ones that stood and said the pledge. That is alarming and makes me feel very sad.

227. I worked very hard and pushed myself to the limits to become Dr. Norris. I like the sound of that.

228. I have taught history for a long time. I have never seen or read about all the sacrifices thousands of White men made to free slaves during the Civil War.

229. I hear school administrators asking, what can we do to improve things in our schools? The answer is: to allow religion, enforce the rules, not allow cell phones, and hold kids accountable for their actions and behavior. However, that makes too much sense.

230. I always encourage my students to challenge me. Sometimes, they are right and other times they have elements of the truth. Perhaps the truth is somewhere in between it all.

231. I often wonder, if we didn't legally force children to attend school, how many would take advantage of America's free public school system. Probably, not too many.

232. As a teacher of history, I have seen people fight over the same things repeatedly. Haven't we had enough death and destruction throughout history?

233. Would you want a C student doing heart or brain surgery on you? That is why you cannot fake higher education.

234. The two things' sports, and higher education have in common are that you cannot fake either one. Once you are on the playing field, you are either able to perform or you are not. I like that.

235. Did you know that less than 3% of the world population has a doctorate degree? You would think with all the educational opportunities available; more people would participate. That tells me two things. One; they don't care. Or two; they are not capable of getting to that point.

236. I always tell my students, instead of trying to show people how cool and tough you are. Why don't you show them how smart you are?

237. I hate to see people waste their talent and potential. That applies to me as well.

238. There is a fallacy that public schools are not well-funded. In fact, they receive much more money than most private schools. However, most private schools outperform public schools. I feel this is due to several factors.

1.) Private schools teach religion.

2.) Private schools typically have more intact families.

3.) Private schools don't have to accept everybody.

4.) Private schools don't have to tolerate bad behavior.

You would think public schools would do what private schools do. It has to do with separation of church and state.

239. Accomplishment means you did what you had to do to succeed.

240. When I was a kid in school you could get into a fight, and after the fight you would both shake hands and apologize. Today, the first thought that comes to mind is lawsuits and revenge.

241. I guess you can say I am a well-educated country boy.

242. I have gained much knowledge from my education but put me on a motorcycle and I am completely happy.

243. I have open and honest discussions with all my students. They like and appreciate that.

244. You will learn something if you just sit down and listen to what I have to say.

245. Unfortunately, intelligence is measured not by the amount of education, but by how successful you are at making money.

246. Most people value education as I do. But many look at how much money you make and disregard how much knowledge a person has. It is always about the money.

247. When I was a student, I would hang on the teachers every word, because I wanted to gain all the knowledge I could. In many of our public schools today, many of the students are more concerned with talking and playing video games then they are at learning anything, or in doing any real work.

248. The work I did to earn my doctorate degree reminds me of doing hard labor, because it was far from easy.

249. I don't have an honorary doctorate degree because I have the real thing.

250. Often, as a teacher, I gave my students notes on the material I would cover in my class, only to see the notes thrown on the floor. When I ask, why? Students tell me they don't care about the notes, and they aren't important. Then I asked, what if I gave you $20.00, would you throw that on the floor? They all said, no. They said the money has value, but school doesn't. I say to them, to earn the money you value, you first need the notes you threw on the floor. They still don't see the connection. And we blame teachers for this attitude.

251. As an educator, I feel I can encourage some students to learn. Hopefully, they see the value it provides to their lives.

252. When we fail one student, in essence, we have failed many.

253. If bad habits can be taught, they can be untaught.

254. I feel being labeled as either a good teacher or a bad teacher is answered by how well we relate to the students we teach. If the students buy into what we are doing, and they see the value in it, then we may appear as a good teacher. If the students don't buy into what we are teaching, then we may be seen as a bad teacher.

255. It is easy to challenge what someone has done before us, because we have the luxury to see their finished product. We may criticize their work to make ourselves appear superior in some manner, when what they produced was most likely brilliant on its own.

256. The more education you have, the less dependent you are upon others.

257. Having clear goals, sound ethics, and being able to create trust will all lead to attainable goals.

258. If I can successfully instruct and lead another person in the proper manner, I have contributed to the success of our nation.

259. I am not going to apologize for being well-educated.

260. I have never seen such high levels of aggression, disrespect, and unmotivated students as I have seen in the last few years. I think our country is in big trouble if these trends don't improve.

261. We need to go back to teaching kids' manners, social skills, and good eating habits, because many parents are not doing the job.

262. As a teacher, I have seen all kinds of students. Students who will do whatever it takes to be academically successful. And others, who will do nothing to be academically successful.

263. I have had some excellent students that I wish I never had to give up. It was a joy to teach them and have them in my class. On the other hand, I have had students that I could easily see will end up in prison.

264. I am seriously concerned about the future of America. Never have I seen so many students who have no interest in learning. Their main objective is to do as little as possible towards their education, and as much as possible to disrupt the students who really want to learn.

265. In America, we should have the option to kick disruptive students out of school. Then we will be left with kids that want to make something of themselves.

266. Perhaps we should charge people to attend public school. This way, they might place more value on education.

SEX AND GENDER

267. For a man, a woman is the greatest gift of all. She can also be his biggest curse.

268. My daddy always said, "Son, a woman can make you or she can break you." Oh, how right he was.

269. There was a day when a man that wore an earring would get beaten up. Today, we cannot often tell the difference between a man and a woman.

270. Did you ever notice as a man and a woman age they start to look more like each other? There is something odd about that.

271. A man that doesn't know his limits is a man who is not a man at all. But a fool, pretending to be a man.

272. I think being a woman is reflected in how she conducts herself. That would be with class, elegance, grace, and style.

273. The beauty, grace, and class of a woman is amazing, but when that falls short, it can be ugly.

274. They say women outlive men. Why is that? Not because they are stronger, but because they know how to handle the weights.

275. You know how beautiful a meal can be to the eyes. Beauty is the same way. But drop that food on the floor and nobody wants it. Beauty is like that; it can be taken as fast as it is given.

276. What is the most romantic thing? Is it the reality of the moment or is it what one remembers from the experience? Interpretation is all that matters.

277. Whenever I want to impress a woman, I just smile.

278. Loving a woman is easy, understanding what she feels is not so easy.

279. Men that go to strip clubs are fools.

280. A real man is a person that has power over another, but never uses it. They allow the weaker one to shine with all the power and potential they have.

281. Men need to be men and women need to be women. That makes too much sense; we can't have that now, can we?

282. My dad taught me a lot about women. I remember looking at a photo of a sexy woman. I told my dad; I don't want one of those. Now I think, how can I have a collection?

283. A woman once told me, I was like a corvette. How's that, I said? She said, "I was long, sleek, and sexy." I will have to agree with that.

284. Love is like the wind, you never know when it will come, and it leaves just as fast.

285. The sound of a high-performance engine is like the sound of a Harley Davidson, sexy.

286. Intimacy between a man and a woman is precious and beautiful. Somehow, society has reduced it to an act where the two people involved may not even like each other. No wonder there are so many divorces.

287. I'm not a fan of tattoos. Why in the world would a beautiful woman take what God has given her and mark it all up? Makes no sense. That goes for the men too.

288. You know what gets me? When an old man has two sprigs of grey hair, ties it in what is supposed to be a ponytail, and decides to add pierced earrings to the mix. Have you looked in the mirror man? That is ridiculous.

289. People say that men make the laws. If that is the case, why do they make laws that completely favor women in terms of divorce and the custody of their children? Are these men really that stupid? I guess so.

290. I think a marriage license should cost thousands of dollars. If that were the case, maybe people would take being married more seriously.

291. If men and women knew coming into a marriage, they would have to share their children equally and pay for them equally, there would most likely be very few divorces.

292. What ever happened to men and women dressing with class and style? Men more suits and women dresses. Like many other things, elegance, class, and style went out the window.

293. I think sexy is taking what you have and making the best of it.

294. A man can have money, power, and fame. But if you don't have a woman of quality at your side, none of it means a thing.

295. I was on a flight once and the stewardess told me, I was an island man. I said, what does that mean? She said, it means that I would like to be on a deserted island with you. At that time, I thought, this sounds good to me.

296. Why do we pretend men are women and women are men? This is not right.

THE WORLD

297. If you have faith for a better world, you will go on.

298. Time waits for nobody, except itself.

299. Hatred is war at its finest hour.

300. Everything in life is simple; people just complicate it due to their own greed and selfishness.

301. Everybody wants the same things in life. To be loved, have a nice job, and a nice home. How we get there is something completely different.

302. I wish I could give everybody what they want, but even then, many would not be satisfied.

303. When the dust settles, we will see how ridiculous all the fighting has been.

304. When life seems too bad to go on, remember the many who have come before us have gone through the same thing, so you are never alone.

305. Peace comes with a price, but nobody has ever decided what price is fair.

306. Peace is the easiest thing to have, but humanity just doesn't get that.

307. Ignorance is always a good excuse to be rude. But what happens when ignorance runs out? I guess we must face the truth. Are we ready to do that?

308. I wish I could meet and get to know everybody. That is impossible, so I try to reach all I can through my words, because there is only one man that can know everybody. I am not that man.

309. When I look at people, I often wonder if they are happy and loved. I wonder what they think of me.

310. The greatest gift I have ever been given is the gift of a smile and a kind word.

311. I don't care if the whole world is against me if I know I am right. There is no shame in doing the right thing.

312. In a way, everybody is weird. But there are some people who are just odd as hell.

313. Just as the sun will rise and set, in some manner, just will prevail in time.

314. Even the worst amongst us has admirers. Perhaps it is the fact they are defiant that intrigues us so.

315. People love violence. We pretend; however, to be civilized.

316. People know the truth, but many are afraid to face it. Then, they must admit they were wrong.

317. The question regarding the fate of humanity is one that people have tried to answer for thousands of years. Instead of trying to answer the question, why don't we take action to improve it?

318. Everybody is even in death. Like the day we were born, we all leave the same way, with nothing.

319. The world they say is what you make it. I say the world is whatever you want it to be. The question is, do you have the courage to do what you chose?

320. When I look at the ocean, I see hope for a better world. Why, you ask? Because it is unknown. That allows us to dream it as we wish it to be.

321. What do evil, hatred, crime, tragedy, and unhappiness all have in common? They are in all of us. Be sure to keep your door locked.

322. What is the most valuable thing of all? Answer: internal peace. Without that, one is like a nomad searching forever, but never finding or knowing what he is looking for. He just keeps searching blindly without direction.

323. I love animals, and I can often see why people place animals over people. I think, if we placed people over animals, the world might be a better place. What do you think?

324. A smile is the one thing that is universal. Boy if we could just figure out how to apply that to all we do, the world would be great.

325. Humanity is one of those things we find when we feel there is none.

326. When things appear to be out of control just slow it all down and let the world catch up with you.

327. Quitters are usually lazy and lazy people are usually quitters.

328. People who dream the greatest make the most noise.

329. Whenever someone says they have no friends, maybe it is because they are not so friendly themselves.

330. Nature is the benchmark to all that is good.

331. Liars, what can I say about these creeps, except shame on you!

332. Who is the most cowardly, terrorists or the ones that harbor them?

333. What does having class, integrity, humanity, and style do for you? Apparently not much, but in my world, it means everything.

334. The world moves on with or without us.

335. People that abuse children? The answer, death. You get the picture?

336. We worry so much about offending someone that we pretend like we don't notice what they do. Are we that ignorant? Apparently, we are.

337. They said rock n roll would never die, but it did. They say we would never put a man on the moon, and we did. They say we will have a nuclear war and we have not. Let's hope that one doesn't come true.

338. Good triumphs over bad. Otherwise, society would collapse.

339. I hope we never discover all the mysteries of space, because if we do, I know we will corrupt it too. Some things are better left untouched.

340. From peace comes resolution. From resolution comes love. From love, we create a better world.

341. I think people love to watch violence in any form. It allows people to vent without the risk of going to jail.

342. You know why so many people have so many problems? Many of them are too lazy to do anything about it.

343. I hate cigarettes. I think the people that smoke them are making a bad decision. We get enough bad things from our air and food. Why add to the problem?

344. I think one of the reasons why many Europeans are admired and vilified is because so many other groups are just jealous of their success.

345. I have found from my travels that most people are more alike than they are different.

346. People ask me, why do I like to write? I say, I am so tired of so many loud mouths that make no sense being given airtime that I feel I must say these things in hope the world will get better.

347. The world seems to pay attention to people with money even if they have no intelligence, morality, or a sense of right or wrong. What is wrong with us?

348. The world's problems appear to be overwhelming, and perhaps they are. Put aside your heartache and latch onto some hope. That will get you through the day.

349. Flowers signify all that is beautiful and peaceful in the world. That is why you should give flowers to the people you love while they are here to enjoy them.

350. Laws keep people in check. Without them, this world would be much more out of control than it already is.

351. You notice when people want money from you, or they want you to buy something for them, how nice they are. Wouldn't it be great if they acted that way even if no money was involved?

352. I would like to be able to teach the world all about love, life, and doing the right thing. I may or may not be qualified, but more than anything, I want this world to be a better place.

353. At times, I feel like I want to say or do nothing about the world. Sometimes it may be best just to go to work, enjoy my family and friends, and let it all be. But if I did that, I would be no different than the millions of people that sit idly by and do nothing at all.

354. If you cannot see what I have said is true, then you must be blind to the truth. Let make this world a better place for all of us.

355. How many people does it take to save the world? Only one, if you save yourself, you have in effect, saved the world.

356. Some days I feel like I can conquer the world. Other days, I feel like the world has already conquered me.

357. Does the universe end? If so, where are we along the continuum? I guess if we knew that, the mystery would be gone. Right?

358. Bad people always get away with too much.

359. Good people always seem to struggle.

360. God bless the world!

THE U.S. AND POLITICS

361. The last time I checked, we still had freedom of speech. However, it has slowly disappeared with many other American values.

362. There are so many things I would love to comment on, but due to my limited freedom of speech, I will pass on that opportunity.

363. So many people have died to give us the freedom to vote in the Unites States. However, when we have elections, less than 50% of the population that could vote, votes. There is something wrong with this mindset.

364. How dare I speak my mind! This is not allowed any more. I can only say what offends nobody.

365. The abnormal has become the normal. I guess in time, the normal will be normal again.

366. Is this what you really want, or are you just too lazy to do anything?

367. Are people who wear tattoos tough, cool, and trendy? Or are they people who are none of those things, just people trying to be those things?

368. I like to do things the old-fashioned way where it took one week to send mail across the country. Now, we can get things in a few seconds. Much like everything, everybody wants it now. Perhaps, later is not so bad after all.

369. If you don't know anything about your government and the people that run it, you are setting yourself up for disaster or worse.

370. Trying to get the government to listen to you is like trying to put a contact lens in a tiger.

371. Whenever you allow welfare to flourish as we have in America, you are disgracing and discrediting all our ancestors fought for, which is life, liberty, and peace. Welfare is neither of those.

372. When one looks at history all empires have fallen. Why do so many people think this will not happen to America. It is that arrogance that caused other nations to fall. Yet, we often ignore all the lessons of history. How dare us!

373. Whenever you place the destiny of your life in another's hand, you are playing fetch with a lion.

374. Bravery is measured in terms of who survives not the ones that paid the price for their glory.

375. When America glorifies killers, porn stars, and strippers, you now can understand, why the world hates us so much.

376. Only in Hollywood can so many with few morals and little talent be so successful.

377. Life was better when moms stayed home, dads worked, kids were concerned about grades and sports. What happened to the American dream? The 60's, 70's, 80's and 90's. And it's getting worse.

378. Many people often talk about war and the price that must be paid for it, but only a few are brave enough to honor that challenge. To them I say, thank you for my freedom.

379. Freedom means many things to different people. But we are never truly free. Laws, money, and limited opportunities restrict everything we do.

380. The greatest thing I ever tasted was free. It was the freedom to be able to choose it that was so delicious.

381. Why does the U.S. Government keep funding war when we have problems here nobody even addresses?

382. TV is one of those inventions that was created to entertain us, but in America, we honor it as if it were some god. How strange.

383. I am for the 2nd Amendment to the U.S. Constitution. However, I wish guns had never been invented. But we would still figure out ways to harm our fellow man.

384. Tradition, I like tradition. However, in America we don't have too many anymore because the liberal left and the biased media have labeled them as oppressive, racist, and discriminatory. Americas traditions are none of those.

385. It seems that all of America's traditions are now imported.

386. Immigration is great if one goes about it the legal way. Only in America can one break the law and then act as if they are the victim of mass discrimination. How dumb we must look to the world.

387. Heroes and their accomplishments seem to loom larger than when they were alive.

388. I am so tired of people that have no intelligence getting so much attention. We seem to crave people who are ignorant. I think it makes us feel better about ourselves. Too bad we can't do that on our own.

389. Sorry, but I don't get the long dirty looking beard thing on many men. Do you like looking like an old man?

390. I don't understand this fascination with tattoos. They add absolutely nothing to a person's appearance. In fact, most gang members, criminals, strippers, and hookers often have them.

391. If people in Hollywood weren't allowed to use the F word there wouldn't be too many TV shows or films made, because there aren't enough talented people to be able to write compelling scripts without using that word. I guess that is why TV Land is so popular.

392. Have you ever noticed the most watched and loved films have no profanity, no nudity, and scripts that have stories instead of a bunch of actors cursing. You would think the powers that be in Hollywood would take notice. After all, isn't the bottom line all they are concerned with?

393. We should have zero tolerance for law breakers. Perhaps then, people might respect the law. I forgot; I am no longer allowed to have any opinions.

394. Violence equals jail. No excuses.

395. Did you know the wages for most jobs have remained almost the same for the last 20 years? Why, because the rich business owners love cheap labor, even if it means selling out fellow Americans.

396. In America we have a very high rate of STD's and single moms. Maybe, they need to spend a little more time in church.

397. I am a Republican, but I started out as a Democrat. Perhaps, it doesn't make much difference.

398. Most people don't know the difference between the two dominant political parties. That's easy to understand, because many people don't even know who the Vice-President of the United States is.

399. I feel one should respect the office of the President of the United States. No matter what your political beliefs.

400. How did America get away with declaring war on Iraq? When, at the time, they did nothing wrong to us. Perhaps it's because we need the oil. I hope they all choke on it.

401. Now that the war in Iraq is over for the United States, Iraq is still not at peace.

402. I would love to be the governor of California, and one day, perhaps even the President of the United States. People would either love me or hate me. That is okay, but I would get things done that would benefit millions, rather than a select group based on race, gender, or orientation.

403. I am an English, Irish, and Polish American, or is it a European American? How about just an American. I like that one best.

404. The town I grew up in reminds me of Mayberry. I sure wish the whole world was like that, but if it were, the news stations would be out of business, because they love chaos and something decent would be too normal.

405. Maybe if we stopped sending financial aid to other countries, we could provide health insurance to our own citizens.

406. Why do we honor and respect athletes so much? I guess it is because they rise above average. Whatever happened to self-respect? I guess it went out the window with the cat.

407. Whenever one assumes a position of power you are both praised and cursed.

408. I would like to lead America back to a simpler way of life.

409. Country music is the soul of America. Once you listen to it, you are hooked.

410. I would have loved to have been a pioneer and been able to see America before it was so full of people. For God's sake, preserve what land we have left, because when it is gone, it is gone.

411. Why did we help people in Afghanistan and Iraq? Many of them hate America. Apparently, our government doesn't know either.

412. I respect the people that have come before me, and I respect the ones yet to come by preserving nature for them.

413. You kids are the future, so be prepared.

414. I really dislike those air blowers that move the leaves and trash around the streets. All they do is move the trash from one spot to another. Get off your lazy rears and use an old-fashioned broom and dump the trash in an old-fashioned trash can.

415. The average person is too busy working to pay the bills to worry about politics and what's going on in society. That's bad for all of us.

416. People need to be a little afraid of the police. Society was a little better when they were.

417. History should tell us all we need to know about what not to do. But we often ignore it, like we ignore our inner thoughts. Because those thoughts usually hold the correct answer.

418. Seat belts are a money-making scheme for local governments. If they cared so much about safety and saving lives buses would have seat belts and motorcycles would not be allowed on the highway and be allowed to drive between the cars with one to two inches between them.

419. Parking tickets help finance local government spending by charging outrageous fines that working people cannot afford. And they get away with it. We are such fools.

420. If you dismiss history, you are dismissing yourself and all that came before you.

421. History repeats itself to some extent. The only thing that changes is the cast of characters.

422. There are almost 400 million Americans. In your lifetime you will not even meet 1% or 4 million of those people. Just think of all the amazing people you will never get to know.

423. I saw the movie called "America" the other day. Finally, a movie that shows what is really going on in the United States. I applaud you!

424. Why do you never see Mexican people trying to sneak back into their own country? Because life here is better.

425. If the war in Iraq was really about oil, then why is the price of oil and gas still so high? We had the chance to dominate the area and provide our country with cheap fuel prices again, but we did not. What does this say about America?

426. How could former President Obama who attended a church with a racist Black pastor be so popular? Answer: most Americans know little about politics, or even care.

427. It really gets me when you have healthy adults standing outside a liquor store all day asking hard working people for money. Get your lazy ass out there and get a job.

428. We have generation after generation on welfare in the United States. The sad thing is they feel entitled to it. Those are some good old-fashioned American values, aren't they?

429. Many Americans love government handouts. Typically, the ones that want it are usually the ones that have done nothing with their life. If they complain enough, the government will reward them for their laziness and lack of success.

430. People complain when the police crackdown on crime. Then, when the police aren't proactive, the community says, they are not doing enough. I say, we need to give the police authority to keep our communities safe. No matter where they are.

431. We have many illegal immigrants in America. Most have broken the law to get here, have no education, and cannot speak English. Then, they act as if there is some mass plot against them. The police will do nothing to them unless a crime has been committed. Now that takes nerve.

432. Affirmative action has openly allowed so many people to discriminated against White people, and nobody does a thing about it. What many people want is for this special privilege to continue, even though we all know it to be wrong.

433. Many people say America is racist, because if people keep saying it is racist it allows illegal immigrants and others to go about their business and not be bothered or challenged.

434. I predict after the dust has settled in Afghanistan and Iraq, we will bring thousands of them to America free of charge, send them to college, and give them government loans to start a business. Meanwhile, we have many Americans that have been here for generations, and we will do nothing for them.

435. The idea of a flat tax makes perfect sense. For example: each person pays 25% of their earned income to the government. It is taken out of your paycheck by your employer. However, we cannot have that because lawyers and the government like it to be very confusing.

436. It is amazing that rappers cannot sing. What ever happened to real talent like Motown? I guess it left with all the other things that had any class.

437. Where has pride in America gone? With the older generations that are slowly dying.

438. We have allowed violence, sex, drugs, and all other types of evil to be aired on television, in films, and on radio. This is why America has so many problems. Are we really that stupid? I guess we are.

439. The great thing about country music is the stories are beautiful, and the people can actually sing. What a novel idea to have singers that can actually sing. Who would have known?

440. No matter how many laws you make, you cannot mandate ignorance and stupidity.

441. It only takes one judge to allow something that is wrong to occur. That still doesn't make it right, but we have a lot of people without any backbone and courage to take a stand. Unfortunately, all of us will pay for that.

442. We have never had true freedom of speech. We are only allowed to say what most people want to hear. That is anything but the truth.

443. Gas prices are criminal. I cannot believe that politicians are not outraged about this. I hope the whole bunch of them are voted out of office.

444. If ghosts and aliens are real, why is it that we have no definitive or clear pictures of any of them? With satellites and cameras everywhere, you would think this would be easy to prove, if it existed.

445. Liberals seem to want to allow anything at all. When will enough be enough? This anything goes attitude is destroying America.

446. The burden of slavery has been the curse of America.

447. It is amazing how many lies parents have told their children about history. When I ask them where they heard that, they say, my parents.

448. I asked my students what they would do if there was a war. Many said they would run to another country to avoid fighting. Apparently, civic duty and love for country have also left the building.

449. When I was a child, the war in Vietnam was raging on. I often fantasized about going there to fight, but it was over when I was only 13. I was too old for Desert Storm and the war in Iraq, but I would still gladly serve my country.

450. World War I and World War II were both fought over natural resources. It looks like World War III is also going to be over natural resources to.

451. America now attempts to create wealth through business and trade instead of through warfare. In some parts of the world, they still haven't gotten the memo.

452. I can completely disagree with another person, but I always allow and respect one's opportunity to speak freely.

453. If you believe it to be true, it is true to you. Even if it's not true.

454. When you allow endless numbers of people to cross America's borders all you are doing is slowly giving away your political, economic, and social power. In time, these people will become citizens and they will vote for their own people.

455. The former mayor of Los Angeles said, we need illegal immigrants to keep the economy flowing. This lie is used as an excuse to allow illegals to flood the nation so it can be taken over through immigration. Americans kept the economy going before all this massive immigration and would have continued to do so.

456. The Asian community typically comes to America and often surpass people who have been here for generations. Perhaps it is better to work hard and stop complaining.

457. At one time, America was almost entirely Native American. Now they are less than 1%. You can see how things change in a short time.

458. How many Native American actors, politicians, and athletes can you name? None, I thought so.

459. Country music, drag racing, and a cold one. Now that's American.

460. When you look at history and the men that have been killed in battle it is reflective of the demographics of the nation at that time of the conflict. It is a lie that Blacks and other minorities have been killed in higher numbers. White men have been killed in greater numbers during war than any other racial group in America.

461. If America wants to be seen as the world's leader, then America needs to conduct itself in a more educated and professional manner. We haven't done that for quite some time.

462. The interesting thing is that people that are not American seem to value what America stands for, more than people who are American. Kind of funny, isn't it?

463. Millions of people risk jail, death, and leave their country to come to America, but the people already in America act as if they are entitled to do as little as possible.

464. I may not agree with how they got here, but I admire the men that stand outside many hardware stores to find work, even if they are here illegally.

465. I get upset when I see perfectly healthy Americans standing alongside a road pretending to be homeless to scam other hard-working Americans out of their money. I think you are a fool if you give them anything.

466. One day, long ago, when I was working in the beverage industry, I needed help. I asked a homeless man to help me. I was going to pay him $30.00 for 2 hours work which is more than I made hourly, at that time, and he said no. I was floored. So, I asked him, why? He said, "I can make more than that standing on a street corner holding up a sign." You have no idea how bad that made me feel that he could stand there and literally take people's money, while I was working hard and paying taxes. Only in America.

467. I love America and I always will but think about it. Why are we allowed to have weapons of mass destruction and other countries are not? It is that arrogance that fuels this hatred towards America.

468. If we had one President and one Congress that would focus on domestic affairs instead of dumping millions of dollars into other countries that most Americans could care less about, and countries that hate us, maybe we could stamp out homelessness and solve our own problems. Isn't that a novel idea?

469. Amongst most politicians, there is arrogance that they know what is best for America. Maybe they do and maybe they don't. However, the difference between them and the rest of us is, they are willing to do what is necessary to get themselves into that position. If everybody were as passionate about what goes on in America, maybe all of us would be better off. What do you think?

470. Our society seems to want to suppress what people can say or write. Sounds a bit like communism to me.

471. I am completely for the death penalty. Why should you be allowed to live if you had the nerve to take another's life while committing a crime? You shouldn't, end of story.

472. We pay too much attention to people that have committed terrible crimes such as: murder or sexual abuse towards children. Does the term hang-em high mean anything?

473. I have traveled to many other countries. The thing I notice in many of them is they promote pride and respect for their nation. Maybe America should take a lesson from them.

474. I could find better looking models walking through a shopping mall than the many I see on TV and in our magazines.

475. You can make a star out of anybody. Just talk about them all the time and people will buy into it.

476. Why is it that on American Idol we only see very young people? Doesn't Hollywood realize that society is aging and there are amazing talents older than say 20 or 21?

477. I wonder what the next phase will be for America's youth, because I don't like the so-called art of tattooing and body piercing.

478. I visited the battlefield of Vietnam in Cu Chi. I could still feel and hear the cries of our lost brothers.

479. Being a gang member, now that's a person with real ambition.

480. If we didn't allow people to flow over our border like water, we would have no unemployment. Yes, Americans are willing to do the work. It is this lie that allows all this illegal immigration.

481. Most people that march in the streets protesting various issues are usually people that have not been successful. The successful people are the ones that are doing the right thing and going to work to support themselves and their families.

482. It used to be that news reporters only gave facts, and rarely stated their opinion. Today, in many cases, it is the opposite. Most of the opinions seem to be anti-American and anti-White.

483. There is the great movement to destroy America from within. Let's do all we can to stop this.

484. If I moved to China, I would be expected to know their language, follow their laws, and adapt to their customs and traditions. But when people immigrate to America, they expect America to adapt to them. It never used to be like that. What has changed? Poor political leaders, lack of pride and no enforcement of America's laws on immigration.

485. Many people around the world have mixed views on America. They seem to either love it or hate it. I hope, if they come to America, they love it and are willing to fight to maintain it.

486. America's jails are full of full of people with broken dreams, broken promises, and broken hearts.

487. If you have pride in yourself and your accomplishments, then you wouldn't care what others think of you.

488. Personally, I don't agree with having women in battle. Although I think they are just as competent, I just don't agree with it.

489. If women really want to be on the battlefield with men, then they need to also shave their heads and be expected to be able to do all that a man can do physically.

490. History will tell us if the decisions in Iraq were correct or not.

491. I don't like having to listen to politicians that know less about the world, the government, and history than I do. But they tell the rest of us what to do.

492. Just like in the late 1970's when we had the so-called gas shortage, we now have an overabundance of oil in the United States, but the lies are continuing.

493. Whenever you are in a position of power you need to do what is best for the people you serve and not what is best for you.

494. If Jerry Springer can have a TV show anybody should be able to have one. Nobody on the show has any talent. What they show to the rest of the world is how ignorant many people are in America. What a disgrace.

495. The American dream. What is it? It used to be Americans hoped to have a loving spouse, children, a decent job, a nice home and be allowed the opportunity to live out their dreams. But somewhere along the way, that has all changed. So, what is it now? I think most people have no idea, because so many will never be able to afford a home or have the chance to be loved. Plus, we have so many broken marriages that many of our children will never know a two-parent family. Maybe if we went back to some basics such as: honoring God, teaching morality, manners, and being neighborly and friendly again maybe things will change, and the American dream will be in sight again.

496. Everybody seemed to blame President Bush for the U.S. being in Iraq. However, after the first 90 days, the president must have approval from congress to keep the troops there. As we know, congress is made up of both democrats and republicans. Funny how the media doesn't mention that. All they did was blame Bush. But the truth is, all of them are to blame.

497. The internet can make anybody a star. All that needs to happen is talk about an individual all the time and before you know it, stardom. Whether you have talent or not.

498. If you look in the dictionary under the word cool. You will find Elvis because there was nobody cooler than him. A true original.

499. Money allows you to buy your way into almost anything, even if you are not qualified.

500. Many American workers are exploited and taken advantage of. However, when we look at the rest of the world, it appears that all of us are rich. However, most Americans struggle to get by every day.

501. Why don't you see that many rappers on American Idol? Answer: because they cannot sing. You cannot fake real talent.

502. You know why the government must bail out financial companies? Answer: because you have a bunch of greedy, self- centered people at the top of the organization. They make more money in one year than their employees will make in a lifetime of working for them. I am not depriving them of their dues, but it would be nice if some of the wealth was spread out a little more evenly.

503. There is nothing more honorable than being a military veteran. I am very proud of all the men and women that served this country. They are truly heroes. But it doesn't give them permission to do nothing with the rest of their life as so many have done after they return home. Perhaps, we should allocate billions of dollars for these heroes rather than sending it to foreign countries.

504. The older I get, the less tolerant I want to be. Why do we tolerate people that do all they can to destroy this nation I will never know.

505. Prison is supposed to be so miserable that nobody would ever want to come back again. But many prisoners live better than the people they victimized. There is something terribly wrong with that.

506. All gangs should be illegal.

507. What happened to American TV? There used to be great shows with talented actors who acted in responsible ways. Today, ignorance seems to rule TV.

508. I still bleed red, white, and blue. Either you love the United States, or you can politely leave.

509. I was born in the USA, and I am proud of it.

510. If America is so terrible and racist due to White people, why do we have millions of immigrants both legal and illegal that desperately want to be in America? Why would anyone come to a nation where they are discriminated against, and continue to remain here if they were? They could remain in their own nation with their own people and be completely immersed in their own culture.

511. When we talk about diversity, what we really mean is no White people.

RELIGION

512. Jesus had no army, no money, and no government backing him. Yet, he is the most adored person that ever lived. So, either he really is the son of God, or he is an absolute genius.

513. Evil men often hide behind God and religion to justify the hatred in their heart.

514. Love like the river must flow, or we are all destined to die of thirst.

515. I am just a man. I wish I were above that, but we all fall short when we look to God.

516. I know God will come back one day. I sure wish today was that day.

517. Religion like politics, everybody thinks they are right.

518. The more I know about life and God, the less I think I know. Perhaps it was better to be in the dark.

519. When I think about God, I drop to my knees, I cry out loud for his love, and tears blanket my face. I love that feeling.

520. I liked it when men were men and women were women. I think God likes it that way too. I have forgotten; we have taken God out of everything. Sorry…on second thought, I am not sorry.

521. Jesus tried to get people to love one another. So, who am I to think I can change things? Nobody I guess, but I must press on.

522. Our court system is not the best, the most just, or fair to all. But one must remember, it is the rule of man, not God, no wonder it is not perfect.

523. We can show kids how to put condoms on in our schools and teach them about the alternative lifestyle of the LGBTQIA+ community, and to hate White people through the hateful rhetoric of critical race theory and diversity, equity, and inclusion, but God and religion; how dare you expose my child to that non-sense. What cowards and fools we are.

524. My heroes are God, my family, and the doctors who have saved me several times.

525. Religion, like any belief only exists in your mind. The reality is different for us all.

526. When I think of God, I often ask him, what can you do for me, Lord? Then I realize, I need to be doing what he wants for me, not what I want for me.

527. I have thought about meeting God. What would I say? I saw him once in my dreams and all I did was bow down and cry. I was speechless. What can one say to perfection?

528. Maybe if people started honoring God, the world might be a better place.

529. Have faith in yourself or nobody else will.

530. Have faith in God, but without faith in yourself, God cannot help you.

531. Even non-believers find God when they reach a dead end.

532. Bad people often hide behind God to justify their behavior.

533. Frustration breeds discontent and discontent breeds' anger. Anger is like the devil. You think it loves you, and then after the damage has been done, you realize how much of a sham it all was.

534. I once thought I would never die. Then, I had health problems. I guess God was trying to tell me, I wasn't immortal. Occasionally, when I think he isn't looking, I still act tough. I hope he didn't see that.

535. I used to ask myself, where have all the good people gone? I found some of them in church.

536. God says the least amongst you is the greatest. I agree with that. However, why don't we honor the least? Because we are hung up on winning, no matter how true his words are.

537. What's more important, your heart or your soul? I say neither. Your heart keeps you going, and your soul comforts your heart. So, what's the answer? Faith.

538. God says, you can move mountains, and I believe that. I say you can't move anything unless you have faith in yourself first. Then, the possibility of moving mountains is endless.

539. What does one plus one equal? Love between you and God. And you thought you knew your math.

540. They say God will come down one day to judge us all. I sure wish that day were today. This world sure needs a waking up.

541. If it were possible, I would love to grant everybody what they wanted. But I am just a man, not God, but even then, I am sure many would still not be satisfied.

542. I am religious, but not weird about it. I feel if we are honoring God, and living a just and decent life, that would please him.

543. I really do love all people. I wish I can bring us all together, but I am unsure as to how to do it. I often ask God to guide me.

544. When I look at the faces of my children, I know that God exists. That is all the proof that I need.

545. God has a room made for you just the way you like it.

546. There is a place like no other. There is no hunger, pain, or sadness. Where you ask? Heaven, but only invited guests are allowed. Are you on the list? I hope so.

547. Without water, there is no life. Without life, there is no death. Without death, there is no heaven. Without heaven, there is only darkness.

548. I think children's eyes are the nearest we get to seeing into the eyes of an angel.

549. The most beautiful, genuine, and precious love is the love that God and our children gives to us so freely.

550. The Bible says that a man should bow down to his wife, and that a wife should look up to her husband. What does that tell you? That God expects us to treat each other with equal respect. It really is that simple.

551. It is amazing how many lies people believe to be true. You can see clearly how Satan has deceived us all.

552. I don't fear Satan because the love of God squashes him like the slug he is.

553. If God pointed out to you what you said, thought, or did to another person was wrong, would you be angry at him? Most likely, not. Would you also admit that you were wrong and attempt never to do it again? I am trying to do the same thing. I hope people get it.

554. People tend to find God when they have completely messed up their life. The good thing is, it's never too late.

555. Too many innocent souls have suffered at the hands of evil people.

556. Jesus had nothing but the cloths on his back and they were taken from him. But he was the richest and wisest man of character, love, and grace. That is why billions believe in him and will follow him forever.

557. No matter what you say it seems to offend somebody somewhere. Even if I say, God bless you. I am still wrong because many people don't believe in God. So, what is a person to do? I say, be as kind and civil as you can to all people. That is the best any of us can do.

558. Many years ago, I was going through a tough time in my life. I was driving down the road, and I said out loud, God, either help me or kill me, and less than 10 seconds later, as I drove over a hill, a truck hit me head on at 55 mph. That forever changed my life.

559. Maybe people need to spend a little more time being nice.

560. Some people are just plain bad. You don't have to get to know them to know this. It is best to stay away from them.

561. Reading the word is reading the word.

562. I hope one day we can all dance in the presence of the Lord.

563. One day, I hope to make it to heaven. Once there, I will know all the answers to my life.

564. Never go against Israel. If you do, you will lose. Fortunately, for the United States, we are allies with Israel.

565. I was raised Catholic. So, you can imagine what my views on marriage are.

566. I wish that I could love like Jesus and be loved like Jesus.

567. The most important book is the Bible.

RACE

568. The more you hate, the smaller you become.

569. Hatred is something we may not see, but we sure feel its presence, even in darkness.

570. Injustice is sometimes real, but often it is what you have created in your mind. The only injustice is what you have done to yourself.

571. We often blame others for our failure, but the truth is there for us to see. We just never open the blinds.

572. People never think about hatred unless it is directed at them.

573. Violence and murder don't solve problems, they brew hate.

574. Racism yields violence whereas peace and recognition protect non-violence.

575. You know what I hate? Hate.

576. Except for Dr. King, most self- proclaimed civil rights leaders do more to tear people apart then they ever do to promote peace between the races. They hide behind what they feel and hate in themselves.

577. Many civil rights leaders look for anything they can remotely tag as racism. I wonder what they would think if someone watched all they said and did?

578. If there is such a thing as White privilege, I sure which I had some, because all I have done and accomplished has been a struggle.

579. Never touch a White man's radio when he is listening to country music.

580. You never see a White man, a Black man, or an Asian man standing in front of Home Depot willing to do anything to make money for his family. And we wonder why America is in the shape it is in.

581. At one time, affirmative action was needed. Today affirmative action is nothing but pure discrimination targeting White people. Sorry, nobody is supposed to know that and if you do, act as if you don't.

582. Republicans have done more for civil rights than democrats, but they don't seem to get any credit. How is that?

583. Whenever you give one group special treatment, you discriminate against another group. So, how do we keep things equitable? You chose the best one for the job.

584. If America is so racist; why does everybody in the world want to come here? Because, we are not, that's why.

585. Many comedians use humor to say what they really think about others, and they get away with it. Perhaps, we should make jokes out of all our insults.

586. White men can dance; just look at the dance shows on TV. What an insult this is.

587. There is much truth to stereotyping and generalizations. However, many people use it as an excuse to alter the facts, and to push their own political and racial agenda, even if they stretch the truth, which they do.

588. The reason many people struggle in life has nothing to do with discrimination, prejudice, or racism. It is often due to their bad choices in life.

589. You can make laws that prohibit hatred, but it only masks the real problem. To really have an impact, we need to teach our children manners, tolerance, and social skills starting from a very young age. Not only at home, but at school, but we fail to do that.

590. Isn't any crime of violence a hate crime? After all, if a person is being raped, robbed, or murdered it is not out of love. Think about that.

591. Why are so many people afraid of people due to their race? Can't we take the time to really know a person?

592. When we look at history, all races and cultures have been both conqueror and victim.

593. The truth about slavery is that Africans sold their own people into it. They are still doing this in many parts of Africa. Why is the media afraid to talk about this? Because the agenda is to always portray Blacks as being victims, and Whites as they oppressor. Black people victimized their own people by selling them into slavery.

594. We have become so politically correct that we cannot honestly address the real issues and problems that face society. Due to the fear of being labeled racist or the fear of losing one's job. So, we all pretend and sugar coat the real issues, and then wonder why we cannot solve our problems.

595. Professional sports aren't about equality. Many great athletes are overlooked due to their race.

596. Many people from Iraq have immigrated to America and they live freely without any harassment, but Americans couldn't go to Iraq and walk down the street, or they may be killed for being an American. And people say America is racist and discriminates. Come on now, that lie has gone too far.

597. I don't care how you attempt to mask it, being in a racist organization tells everybody all about you. That you are a person that is full of deception, and your agenda is only to serve members of your own race.

598. Black people used to feel guilty for being Black, now White people feel guilty for being White. Why can't all of us just be proud of who we are?

599. They say that minorities in Los Angeles get pulled over more often than Whites. That is true, because there are very few Whites living in those cities. You see how people take facts and misuse them to victimize minorities and demonize Whites.

600. Let's not pretend to be what we are not. It is okay to be who you are.

601. I hate the word minority because it implies some sort of inferiority, which it isn't. All it really means is there aren't as many of you as there are of other races.

602. Living in California, I am a minority for being White. That doesn't bother me. Like all people, I hope my culture, language, and religion are acknowledged.

603. Acknowledgement, recognition, and compassion, isn't that want everybody wants?

604. America seems to be moving towards equality and equity at any costs. Whether it's affirmative action, special entitlement programs, or lowering the standards for college entrance exams and other areas of employment. One way or the other, we are going to have things equal, even if we need to lie, alter facts, and discriminate against White people.

605. I lost a job once and I took a job doing hard labor. One man said, what are you doing here? You look too smart to be at this job. I said, I could care less about that. I have two children to support and my love for them wouldn't allow me to go a day with making money for them.

606. There is this mindset that we need to do all we can to get White people out of power, at any cost. And when that happens, the new people in charge are going to say, it's our turn now. You have had it for over 300 years. Think I am wrong?

607. Before I knew much about history, when I was young and dumb. I thought Dr. King was just a troublemaker. Then, as I grew older, and I studied more about history I realized how intelligent, great, and unique he was.

608. Did you know the first man to own a slave in America was a Black man? His name was, Anthony Johnson. Why are facts like this left out?

609. In America less than 5% of the White population owned slaves. In fact, there were as many Black people that owned slaves as Whites. Why are these facts left out of the history books?

610. America is no longer Black and White. It is a mixture of the entire world.

611. When you look at history, the minority is always trying to dethrone the majority.

612. Everybody wants to rule the world. I guess it's just human nature. I wish we can all rule the world together.

613. Forgive me if I have offended you. I am for the civil rights of all people.

614. The hatred in your heart, will in time, destroy you.

615. Many of my students thought I wasn't Caucasian. I can't understand that. I surely look Caucasian. Maybe it's because I'm different than the stereotypes they have about White people.

616. Many students have asked me, why we have not had a Latino President. I say, one day we will, and everybody clapped. You can clearly see that people want their own people to be in charge.

617. Many of my students have misconceptions about White people. They said I was different than they thought I would be. What is that supposed to mean? I guess it means White men aren't so bad after all.

618. Many people are so uncomfortable about their race. I wish we could all be comfortable just being who we are. Wouldn't that be nice?

619. So many people give others fake respect to avoid losing their jobs.

620. Many talented people get overlooked due to affirmative action, quotas, and political correctness.

LIFE

621. Dreams, like the wind change directions all the time. That is why it is important to be adaptable.

622. Everybody is even in death.

623. Death doesn't discriminate. One day, it knocks at the door.

624. What you carry in your heart is the direction your life will follow.

625. Peace is the easiest thing to have, but humanity just doesn't get that.

626. I am never bored because life gives me more to do than I have time for.

627. I never think about my own demise. I worry about the ones that I leave behind. There is never enough time to share with them.

628. Life is just as simple as it is complicated. I choose the simple path. I must have gotten lost or made a wrong turn somewhere. I wish I knew where. Perhaps, I am so lost I will never find the road home.

629. Time is our own, use yours like each second was your last, because one never knows when the last second will tick away.

630. Why don't people live in the moment. The moment is what's important, not what may happen next. Often, there is no next.

631. Tomorrow may come, but today is what permits tomorrow.

632. Our lives may wither in time, but time disappears in a second.

633. I keep asking myself, am I good enough yet? Then I realized, I am what I am. I guess that is good enough for me. I may never please the world.

634. Murder, how dare someone think they have the right to take a person's life. Only the course of time has that right.

635. What's more beautiful, to be young or old? Both are at the opposite end of life's spectrum. For the young, the journey has just begun, and for the old, the journey is almost over. Perhaps, we should enjoy the trip and not think about where it begins or ends.

636. When I look into the mirror, I realize one can never beat time.

637. I hope I am not forgotten.

638. People spend too much time thinking about what they would like to do. By the time they decide, the window is most likely closed. Don't let that happen to you.

639. Negativity never allows kindness to enter.

640. Stop complaining, one day you won't be here to complain.

641. Wasting time is like wasting money. One day, you say, where did it all go?

642. We try to avoid traffic, but look at the bright side, it allows us to be alone and have time to think.

643. Stop worrying about the decisions you make. Once you do that, you can lose the stress that it creates.

644. How can something be beautiful and ugly at the same time? Beauty brings joy when it acknowledges you, and beauty brings ugliness when it ignores you.

645. Enjoy your youth because it disappears like a thief in the night.

646. People mistreat us because we allow it.

647. Tomorrow brings one more chance to get it right. Even if it's right already. Are we ever satisfied?

648. The game is never over. Our journey continues even in death.

649. Our legacy is something we think of, but creating it is something beyond our control. What others do with our deeds is something we will never know.

650. The great thing about aging is that you can see all the things you thought were once right were perhaps not so right after all.

651. Riding a motorcycle gives you freedom to dream. Everybody deserves that occasionally.

652. What do we all want? Good health, a decent home, a good job and somebody to love us.

653. Loneliness leads to depression and depression leads to loneliness.

654. You are only as hindered as you think you are.

655. Fear is something I don't know. But being scared, that is something else.

656. Don't dismiss your failures, because to do that, would deny your existence.

657. I better write, because one day I will be too old to write. I guess then, I will just think about all I have done. I hope I can still do that.

658. Life teaches us more about what we don't want, rather than what we do want.

659. Good always prevails over evil; otherwise, society would collapse.

660. Growing up in the country, I thought I had missed a lot. Then I realized, I didn't miss anything. Life was good right where I was.

661. Many days I asked myself. How did I end up here? Then I realized, I am where I am supposed to be that day. It's all a learning process.

662. I am like a lion because I have used a few of my 9 lives.

663. Writing is the one thing that lasts forever.

664. Never joke about having a head on collision. I used to do that until I had one. I am lucky to be alive.

665. When young people die, it really upsets me. There is nothing worse than taking someone's youth.

666. Life is like a party. It's fun while it lasts, but when the party is over all that is left is the mess and an empty room. It is funny how quickly it changes.

667. If your neighbors knew all you thought about them, nobody would get along.

668. The toys of our youth will forever be the toys of our youth.

669. Rejoice young man for being young, growing old maybe a journey, but none of us want to get there too quickly.

670. I hate the cold, but occasionally I need to shiver. It makes me respect being comfortable again.

671. Whenever you retract your words, you dismiss yourself.

672. Everything you do contributes to who you are.

673. The most important thing in your life, other than your health, is your financial situation.

674. Admitting you are wrong is one of the bravest things one can do.

675. Time is the one thing that cannot be controlled, it moves on with or without you.

676. The grades you earn in school reflect what kind of worker you will be during your lifetime.

677. Being young is beautiful, but young people don't realize it until their youth is gone. Then they spend the rest of their lives trying to recapture their youth.

678. Cooperation is a conscious decision where you decide to get along with the other person.

679. Determination is great, but being too determined often means we miss what is under our nose.

680. The chapters of our life are always being written.

681. In time, everything works out. However, in the meantime, you must deal with the pain.

682. Fame is temporary, but honest hard work is something one can be proud of at any age.

683. If you need to think for a long time about whether you should do something, most likely, you should not do it.

684. Being self-sufficient=success.

685. Whenever one assumes a position of power you are both praised and cursed. That applies to many areas of life.

686. Friendship, like everything has limits and conditions. When these boundaries are compromised, it is a test as to the strength of the relationship. Sometimes, the friendship can recover and other times it cannot.

687. Positive thinking has no boundaries.

688. People talk about their choices and the destination these choices have taken them. I believe, we end up where we are supposed to be. Otherwise, you discredit your own existence.

689. Goodbyes are difficult. Even when you leave, your presence is felt by the integrity and character you have left.

690. I think people should assume responsibility for themselves and not look at others to blame.

691. Value life, God, family, and friends. What else does this world have to offer? Nothing.

692. Everything you do in your life follows you.

693. Everybody must conserve nature, without it, nothing else can happen.

694. I don't like the sound of a ticking clock because each second that ticks away brings me closer to my own demise.

695. You are content when you find inner peace.

696. Bravery is measured in terms of who survives, not the ones that paid the price for their glory.

697. Nature always comes back to the beauty it once was.

698. The difference between humans and nature is nature is always what it presents itself to be, and people are sometimes what they present themselves to be.

699. If you want to know why the world is what it is read some history books. It's amazing what you might learn.

700. I tell my students bad things can happen anywhere. Don't live your life in fear, or you may never truly enjoy life.

701. People need to think about their choices instead of rushing into a decision. There would be so many fewer problems.

702. As long as the sun will rise, there is always hope for a better tomorrow.

703. If I have made a mistake, please forgive me. I always try to do the best I can do. I try to be fair and honest to everybody in the process.

704. As long as your heart keeps beating, you will go on.

705. If you knew you were going to die today, what would you do? I would look into the eyes of everybody I loved and ask them to remember how much I loved them until the end.

706. Preserve nature at all costs.

707. Life is like having friends over for dinner. You serve only the best you can offer them. If we treated everybody that well just imagine how wonderful our world would be.

708. Where have all the good people gone? Perhaps, they are right next door, but we aren't neighborly anymore.

709. When you ask yourself, am I a good person? You must first be able to admit who you are. If you can admit that, then you have some hope to better yourself.

710. Being hungry is good, because when you are hungry, you are at your best.

711. Most things I didn't want to happen in my life, have happened in my life. I sure hope I am never rich.

712. Anybody can buy a beautiful car, but creating it out of nothing, that is something magical and special.

713. Beauty and love live forever. Never let yourself get old.

714. Your body may age, but your soul never ages.

715. I always hang in there until the end, because you never know the end of the story until the book is closed and the game is over

716. Does giving flowers to our dearly departed bring joy to them or bring some relief to us? I think, the later.

717. People are always trying to love others like they feel they should be loved, instead of loving the person like they want to be loved.

718. It is harder to recognize the love that is close to us, but it is easier to recognize the love that is far from us.

719. Sometimes the dream of love or what love might be is stronger than the love that is right in front of us. I guess in many ways, we are all dreamers.

720. Honesty is something we all carry in us. Deciding how to use it is something completely different.

721. All of us need waking up from time to time.

722. The only justification for taking another's life is war, the result of a police action, or in self-defense.

723. I wish everybody had the opportunity to be fully and completely loved by another person.

724. Every man changes under pressure.

725. I feel bad for our children. As adults, we are supposed to protect their innocence and guide them to live a proper and fulfilling life. Yet, we have parents that freely use the F word in front of their children. Have numerous sexual partners come in and out of the home, and then we scratch our heads and wonder, how and why our children act and think as they do. Some people just don't deserve to be parents.

726. It doesn't matter if something is true or not. If you say it long enough, many people will believe it to be true.

727. Admiring beauty is one thing but being beautiful takes on many forms.

728. Society is so wasteful. Many people waste their youth on drugs and alcohol. We waste the knowledge of the elderly. Wouldn't it be nice to value all these things?

729. What does it take to be a hero? Doing the right thing, even if it costs you.

730. Time is like a river. It keeps moving much faster than we can keep up with.

731. Life's precious moments happen a few seconds at a time.

732. Everything in life is borrowed, because we take nothing of what we earned or accomplished with us in death.

733. Stop whining and think of all you can accomplish today.

734. If you don't do anything with your life, don't blame society. You need to look into the mirror and point your finger at yourself, because everybody can make something out of themselves if they want to.

735. Accomplishment means you did what was necessary to succeed.

736. Even if I have nothing, I still have all that I have experienced and learned.

737. By not planning you have set yourself up for failure.

738. As one ages, they embrace history more, because they realize, they are now a part of it.

739. What does love mean? It means someone is giving you permission to enter their life and get to know them. By allowing that to occur, love is now possible.

740. Sometimes you are in so deep there is just no turning back.

741. Whatever it was, is now gone. Whatever it is-is the reality we must face. Whatever tomorrow may bring is full of endless possibilities.

742. They say you are paid what you are worth. I don't believe that. The value of each life is worth millions, but society has categorized us based on education, income, and abilities.

743. A person should strive to be their best. That includes both academically and professionally. One should also maintain their health and their youth. But many people obviously don't get that. I think many go out of their way to look their worst and do as little work as possible. And then they wonder why they haven't gotten anywhere in life. I just don't understand that.

744. Nature is the backdrop to everybody's life.

745. You have many women that kill their unborn children or abandon them. And on the other side, you have women that beg God to allow them to have children.

746. It amazes me people pay hard earned money to buy cigarettes, which contributes to their own death. I just don't get that, and I never will.

747. Many people talk about greatness but ignore their potential for greatness.

748. At the end of your life, you are the result of the choices you have made during your life.

749. We should value Earth because we will forever be a part of it.

750. A balanced life leads to a healthy and fulfilling life.

751. Sometimes you don't always end up where you want to be.

752. You know what rocks my world? Rolling down the road in a 1,000 horsepower Corvette and listening to country music with my wife at my side. Life doesn't get much better than that.

753. Whenever I see a car, I cannot have of afford, I tell myself, they are storing it for me. That makes me feel a little better about not having it.

FAMILY

754. Everybody has a father, good, bad, or gone. But to be a dad, that is what it means to be a real man.

755. Without the love of one's family, a man is not complete.

756. When I think about home, I look to my thoughts. They are always with the ones I love. That is where my home is.

757. My work is just my work. My real life begins when I am at home with loved ones.

758. When I think of my children, I still see them as little girls even though they are all grown up.

759. My grandma used to say, you better conserve water. Everybody said, what does that old lady know? That old lady was right.

760. When a man looks at his wife, he should worry about lost time with her instead of thinking about how to love her more. That is what counts, not what has never happened.

761. When I used to look at my ex-wife, I thought, what I treasure I had, only to find out that I was left with fool's gold.

762. My daddy used to get mad at me for no reason. Now, he's not here anymore. I wish I had one more chance to make him mad again.

763. I used to think I was a tough guy, and at times, I still do. Now, I realize it's not the toughness of my exterior that prevails, but it is the softness of my soul that gives me the greatest peace.

764. I miss my dad, but we never really talked much. Maybe, it's the hope that we could be best buddies that I longed for. I sure wish I had that chance again, even if I did get yelled at.

765. I remember my dad saying, "I think of my dad everyday boy. Treat them good son. They are not here long." Yeah dad, I know what you mean now.

766. My sister and I live far away from each other. I wish it were different, but I still have my memories of us as children.

767. My dad was like an old grumpy dog many a day. I used to aggravate him just to hear him bark. That makes me sad, but his bark meant he loved me, even if it wasn't what I expected from him. At least he was there, that is more than I can say for many a dad.

768. We play too much with our children. We need to give them caring discipline. If not, we are doing a great disservice to them.

769. Both of my grandmother's always had a smile and a warm meal for me. I surely miss them.

770. I think my dad would have been a pioneer if he had the chance. But he was too much of a man to just run away.

771. My mom is very old fashioned. That used to bother me. Now I see how beautiful she always was.

772. Nothing sounds as good as a Harley or a hot rod. Except maybe my wife and children saying they love me.

773. Whenever my dad was a bit frustrated, he would say, "Kiss Kate's ass." I would say, what does that mean? He would say, "never mind boy."

774. One of my greatest regrets is not having more time with my daughters. That one thought brings me more sadness than anything else.

775. My ex-wife learned a lot about American culture. She can play the blame game very well.

776. It was fun teaching my ex-wife English, but when we divorced, she pretended as if she never spoke a word of it.

777. No mail today. Means, no bills today. (Mom)

778. Yake a my hiney. (Grand mom)

779. Why is it that men have little say concerning their children if they are not married to the child's mom? She may not allow him to see his child, but she will take his hard-earned money in the process. There is something terrible about that.

780. It takes two people to make a child, and it takes two people to raise a child. Don't mess with God's plan of perfection.

781. I still can see grandpa sitting there making that delicious home-made ice cream. That was the good stuff.

782. One of my grandmothers (Gammy) used to let me sit on her lap as she rocked me to sleep. It was nice being a kid.

783. Go to sleep. (To my wife and children)

784. Bath, bottle, and bed. (To my children)

785. To my wife and children. Always know I love you. Even if we are apart.

786. I told my family, I wanted to write a family cookbook. They all laughed and said, "You don't cook." I said, that's the beauty of it.

787. I have had many jobs in my life and most likely will have many more. But the most rewarding job I ever had is being a dad. That job, I wish I can do forever.

788. The more knowledge you have about raising children, the less dependent you are upon others.

789. One of my dearest friends told me, "You are still a warrior, but sometimes you must put your stick down." (Chris)

790. Some days I feel like I am nobody and that I have accomplished nothing, even though I have accomplished much. Then I realized, I am somebody to my family and friends. This is all that matters to me.

I LOVE TO GO FAST!
NOTHING RULES THE ROAD LIKE A CORVETTE!

I BELIEVE IT IS TIME FOR MY CLOSEUP.

I will always be a cowboy.

God Bless America!
Dr. Mark D. Norris

THE END

www.ingramcontent.com/pod-product-compliance
Lightning Source LLC
Chambersburg PA
CBHW070813170726
48000CB00017B/868